#OPEN TEXTBOOK **tweet**

Driving the Awareness and Adoption of Open Textbooks

By Sharyn Fitzpatrick
Foreword by Wayne Mackintosh
Director, OER Foundation

Published by THINKaha™, an imprint of Happy About®

20660 Stevens Creek Blvd., Suite 210
Cupertino, CA 95014, USA

First Printing: August 2010
Paperback ISBN: 978-1-61699-004-6 (1-61699-004-X)
eBook ISBN: 978-1-61699-005-3 (1-61699-005-8)
Place of Publication: Silicon Valley, California, USA
Paperback Library of Congress Number: 2010927956

Trademarks

Warning and Disclaimer

Advance Praise

"Sharyn Fitzpatrick and Happy About have captured the what and why of open textbooks in a format that will appeal to those who love books and those who love Twitter.

Electronics, computers, telecommunications, and the Internet have driven the cost of reproducing textbooks to zero. These textbooks are still enormously expensive to write, illustrate, design, edit, and market. Open textbooks address both of these market realities.

Open licensing allows professors and instructors to tailor textbooks to their students and to freely mix materials from many open sources. Market models similar to those for open-source software permit both low prices for students and sustainable profits for the creators of the textbooks.

This book explains these principles and many more in today's breezy style."

Jacky Hood, Director, Community College Open Textbooks Collaborative

Acknowledgments

Judy Baker *@educ8ter*, Dean of online learning and technology at Foothill College

---

Bill Buxton, Reviews Manager, College Open Textbooks

Geoff Cain *@geoffcain*, Director, Instructional Design, College of the Redwoods

---

Tom Caswell *@tom4cam*, Founder, Dynamic E-Learning Strategies, Inc.

Erik Christensen, P. E. Chair, Natural Science Department; Professor of Physics, South Florida Community College

---

Sandy Cook, System Director Distance Learning, Kentucky Community and Technical Colleges System (KCTCS)

Una Daly, Associate Director, College Open Textbooks

Muvaffak Gozaydin, Founder, GLOBAL ONLINE Universities Consortium

---

Cable Green *@cgreen*, Director of eLearning & Open Education, Washington State Board for Community and Technical Colleges

---

Andrea Henne, Dean, Online and Distributed Learning, San Diego Community College District

---

Phyllis Hillwig, Ed.D., Chief Operating Officer, Words & Numbers

---

Jacky Hood, Director, College Open Textbooks

Barbara Illowsky, Professor, De Anza College

Tim Lenz, Professor, Special Assistant to the Dean of the College of Arts and Letters for Teaching Initiatives, Florida Atlantic University

---

Mitchell Levy *@HappyAbout,* Marketing Chair, College Open Textbooks; CEO, Happy About, Inc.

Wayne Mackintosh *@Mackiwg,* Founder of WikIEducator and Director, OER Foundation

---

Federico Marchetti, Instructor, Shoreline CC & N Seattle CC

Barbara Mauter, University of Toledo

Lisa McDonnell, JD, PhD, Associate Professor-Social Sciences; PTK Advisor, St. Petersburg College/Seminole/ECampus

---

Clare Mortensen, Research Associate, Institute for the Study of Knowledge Management in Education

---

Paul Orlando *@porlando*, Co-founder, Chatfe

Monica Sain, Foothill Global Access

Jeff Shelstad, Founder and CEO, Flatworld Knowledge

Jeffrey Slebodnick, Professor, Oakland Community College

Liz Yang Tadman, College Open Textbooks Ning manager

Why We Crowdsourced This Book

Open textbooks are fast becoming an integral part of the education road map because the content can be reused, remixed, redistributed, and more. The possibilities for open textbooks and open education resources are limited only by our imagination of what we can create and provide for the future. The communities of dedicated and passionate evangelists that have contributed tweets to this book are advocates for redefining the way students and faculty collaborate and enhance learning, enabling open textbooks to become tools that augment the learning experience for all.

This collection of crowdsourced bite-sized tweets answer key questions from the view of the author, the student, the audience, the college or university who might support open textbooks, and the future of the open textbook movement. Their shared wisdom and advocacy offers us guidance on a path we are all traveling together.

Sharyn Fitzpatrick *@themarcomguru*

About College Open Textbooks

The Community College Open Textbook Collaborative or College Open Textbooks, funded by The William and Flora Hewlett Foundation, is a collection of colleges, governmental agencies, educational nonprofits, and other education-related organizations that are focused on the mission of driving the awareness and adoption of open textbooks. This includes providing training for instructors adopting open resources, peer reviews of open textbooks, and mentoring online professional networks that support for authors opening their resources, and other services.

The initiatives and leadership of College Open Textbooks are driven by member organizations including the Foothill-De Anza District, California Community Colleges Chancellor's Office, Carnegie Mellon University, Community College Open Education Resources, Connexions, Florida Distance Learning Consortium, The Orange Grove, Happy About, Inc., Institute for the Study of Knowledge Management in Education (ISKME), League of Innovation, MERLOT, Open Education Resources Center for California, Textbook Media, and Words & Numbers. For more information and access to available open textbooks, go to http://www.collegeopentextbooks.org.

Driving the Awareness and Adoption of Open Textbooks

Contents

Foreword by Wayne Mackintosh

Mark Twain remarked that he could never "make a good impromptu speech without several hours to prepare it." A tweet, restricted to 140 characters, is a reflection of the impromptu conscience of digital society today. This collection of micro contributions from educators, administrators, and learners reflecting on the burgeoning phenomenon of open education resources and open textbooks is reason to celebrate: we are returning to the core vocation of education, which is to share knowledge freely. Clearly these contributors have thought deeply about the value of "sharing to learn," but more importantly "learning to share."

This book is insightfully clever because it conveys a powerful message that will be a catalyst to nurture and evolve into a growing community of educators worldwide that is committed to the evolution and collaborative planning of education projects rooted in the foundations of open content. It is clear that OER futures are inevitable. After reading this text, I wonder when we look back at the history of these sustainable education futures, will we wonder why it took so long?

Wayne Mackintosh,
Founder of WikiEducator and
Director, OER Foundation

Section 1

What Is Open?

Open is defined as accessible to all, free from limitations, boundaries, or restrictions. The growing trend towards adopting open content is just one piece of the puzzle. It is part of a bigger trend where student and faculty participate in choices that drive customizable learning.

1

No paper was used to produce this
plug for open textbooks—just a few
electrons were rearranged.

2

David Wiley says it best with
4 R's—Reuse, Redistribute, Revise,
and Remix.

3

Open is fundamentally about open licensing. Open is the legal right to reuse, revise, remix, and redistribute.

4

Open means availability at a reasonable cost, regardless of ethnicity, religion, nationality, gender, language, or socioeconomic status.

5

No headaches or worry about using and modifying high quality educational resources to meet learning goals.

6

Open education resources, including open textbooks, are designed to improve teaching and learning.

7

Open means flexible, free, and accessible (flexible formats, nonrestrictive licenses, no to low cost, and available to anyone).

8

Open is freedom—freely modifiable and available, not shackled by restrictive copyright.

9

Open education is a class act.

10

In a wide range of disciplines, open textbooks are available to download and print in various file formats online from web repositories.

11

Open textbooks can range from public domain books to existing textbooks to textbooks created specifically for OER.

12

Open textbooks help solve the problem of the high cost of textbooks, book shortages, and access to textbooks for interactive learning.

13

Open means never having to say you're sorry when you remix and reuse content because you respect the copyright license.

14

Open is a way to significantly reduce the student cost of education, especially textbooks.

15

Open is a way to deliver education to students who struggle to afford it since textbooks are expensive.

Section II

Why Author an Open Textbook?

Textbooks often go out of print, and content is not updated with new editions. Authoring an open textbook opens doors to improved content, longevity, recognition amongst peers, and new professional opportunities.

16

Open textbooks can fundamentally transform and unlock education by actively engaging all of us in the creation of our own learning content.

17

To impact the flat world. To allow others to improve it and extend its reach.

18

To surf the wave of the future, taking digital publications one step further and bringing open access works into a peer review process.

19

Our government should re-route financial aid for expensive commercial textbooks by funding the creation of high quality open textbooks.

20

To author an open textbook is to give something back, to replenish the pool of education from which we ourselves have drunk so deeply.

21

Authoring an open textbook is a good approach to getting published and giving back to the community of educators and students.

22

So we can provide struggling students with a way to purchase expensive texts for a more realistic and empowering price.

23

It provides opportunity for educators to create and share best practices in teaching and learning and contributes to the entire community.

24

When I write an open textbook, I get to benefit from the wisdom of the crowd as they use and adapt the work and share alike.

25

Because that's how science and knowledge have always been communicated.

26

It gives us, as authors, the opportunity to create learning materials that can be readily updated and improved when and how we choose.

27

It is great professional development for the author, and the textbook is improved from the feedback of 50+ adopters worldwide.

28

Pass on the gifts given to you.
Leave a legacy.

29

Open textbooks allow a return to a
free exchange of ideas.

30

Because your textbook will have its own freedom (having reached the age of majority), and it will never go out of print.

Section III

Why Adopt an Open Textbook?

Why not? It is a win-win for students who struggle to afford the high cost of textbooks and faculty who successfully collaborate with their peers to enhance the learning experiences of their students with rich, customized content.

31

OER unleashes the potential for us all to collaborate at the heart of the educational endeavor: sharing knowledge freely.

32

Open textbooks can fundamentally transform and unlock education by actively engaging all of us in the creation of our own learning content.

33

First, because it is good. Second, control over content and revisions. And finally, equal access for all.

34

The academic advantages of open textbooks are found at collegeopentextbooks.org, collegeopentextbooks.ning.com, and your institution of learning.

35

Open access is not just a different format; it changes the way you teach and the way students learn. It is time to reinvent the textbook.

36

To move the market away from expensive commercial textbooks to openly licensed textbooks. This will help to redefine the market.

37

We collectively moved the classifieds from newspapers to craigslist. Now we have the power to do the same with textbooks. We are the market.

38

Open textbooks should be adopted for their quality, affordability, adaptability, portability, scalability, and accessibility.

39

As a professor, I can show students how to be academically successful using open textbooks even if they are financially challenged!

40

Walk the talk about helping others reach their academic goals. Adopting open textbooks shows them that we listened and took action.

41

To work in a collaborative learning community to reduce barriers to education and share and improve learning materials.

42

So students don't have to choose between paying for rent and food and buying expensive textbooks. They need to have more purchase options.

43

As a professor, I vow to do something to relieve the tremendous financial hardships that purchasing expensive textbooks has on my students.

44

As a professor, adding open textbooks adds rich content to my class and decreases the financial hardship that my students struggle with.

45

My students were asked to comment on the free online textbook, and they absolutely loved it! 99% of the comments were positive.

46

Peace of mind is an important benefit of open resources; instructors can quit worrying about copyrights and spend their time teaching.

47

Now we can remix and customize to the learners, providing for a richer learning environment and reducing the cost of content to students.

48

It puts the instructor in full control of all course resources without being tied to having to teach things as presented in a textbook.

49

The ability to modify textbook material and seamlessly integrate it with lectures, class activities, labs, and assignments is priceless.

50

Being in control of your course material with a dynamic textbook significantly increases the joy and personal satisfaction of teaching.

51

Today's economy demands that we do everything we can to keep education open and accessible to all students. Open texts open doors.

52

Because it is open to your contribution as well. You adopt it, you enrich it, and everybody has won.

53

Adopting an open textbook is cheaper than adopting a puppy.

54

Research suggests
that open textbook use
impacts pedagogy by
facilitating student-teacher
interaction and peer-based
learning models.

55

Markets require demand;
instructors need to stop
waiting for perfection and
start adopting from the
five hundred existing
open textbooks.

Section IV

How to Adopt an Open Textbook

Engage a community of
thought leaders who can share
best practices and knowledge.

56

A five-minute flip test and focused reading on a few key content areas will give you a sense of how usable it will be for your class.

57

We start by getting rid of our "not invented here" attitude regarding others' content and move to "proudly borrowed from there."

58

Tell your administrators why you want to adopt an open textbook, join with others in the OER movement, build support, and overcome barriers.

59

Complete a peer review of a textbook. If it matches course curriculum and instructional goals, adopt it and become an in-house advocate.

60

Advocate that open source material that has been peer reviewed often has the same, if not better, quality than printed textbooks.

61

Accessible open textbooks make learning better for a diversity of learners.

62

There are many repositories
for open textbooks such as
MERLOT and Connexions
that have peer-reviewed
textbooks available
for download.

63

Define your criteria for adopting an open textbook. Analyze the content quality and understand how you could integrate it into your class.

64

Adding your own material is also a way to personalize your class and keep information even more up-to-date than the actual textbook itself.

65

Use resources like collegeopentextbooks.org to find and adopt open textbooks.

66

Help the faculty understand that no textbook can replace their experience and understanding of their students.

67

Find a good one, and if there's none, write one yourself.

68

Take advantage of the advance search capabilities of search engines like Google to find open licensed content.

69

Industry research indicates open textbook adoption requires institution-wide support including faculty professional development.

70

Find it, read it, vet it, use it.

71

Think about offering more accessible learning options to encourage change in how we adopt learning for different student needs.

Section V

Why Should Your College/University Care?

Increasing costs, economic challenges, and the new face of learning will impact your university. They need to understand why and how to plan for their future.

72

Equal access to high quality content is a game changer—because legislators, parents, and students care about costs. So why not?

73

Using open educational resources— and contributing to them—requires significant change in the culture of higher education.

74

Colleges need to change their thinking about content as a common resource whose rising tide raises all boats when shared.

75

Because these are part of a growing movement towards education affordability that makes sense and is strongly endorsed by the President.

76

As educators, our goals
should be to do whatever
we can to make educational
opportunities available
and affordable to every
student we can.

77

To offset revenue and margin loss, campus bookstores can provide advice and print-on-demand facilities for open textbooks.

78

Even instructors who cannot find a suitable open textbook benefit when others adopt; students can then afford to take more classes.

79

There are more than twenty open textbook stakeholder groups: teachers, students, colleges, bookstores, libraries, parents, taxpayers, etc.

80

Colleges/universities should care because use of open textbooks can lower educational costs for students.

81

Learning more about open education resources can improve content of online materials and courses.

82

Adoption of open textbooks can have a significant positive impact on overall student persistence, retention, and enrollment.

83

With the cost of textbooks now often exceeding the cost of tuition, open textbooks offer a welcome relief to financially strapped students.

84

This may make college more affordable for new students, which may encourage new enrollments in additional classes they can now afford.

85

The benefits of open textbook adoption include a cost savings for the student, better student success, and an improved bottom line for them.

86

For many, money closes doors to education. Open textbooks open doors.

87

Student cost is a big factor. But also crucial: knowledge spreads better and faster if it is free (as in speech, not only as in beer).

88

Open textbooks open minds!

89

Students interviewed by researchers indicate that portability and reduced cost are the key benefits of open textbook use.

90

The purpose of
education is to educate
all the best it can.

Section VI

How Does the Student Benefit?

Bottom line, it is about the students and offering them affordable options.

91

Students benefit through equal access, affordability, and choice. They can now match learning style to purchase options.

92

It's about economics and academics. Open access promotes active/ interactive learning.

93

Students save money and can contribute to the next version of the open textbook.

94

Students benefit now from educational affordability and later by having high quality educational resources available to review at any time.

95

They save money and help protect our planet by using books that don't end up being out of date in a decade and just end up in a landfill.

96

By providing PDFs that students are allowed to download and edit, much paper—and thus trees— can be saved on the planet.

97

The bottom line—cost is very important to all students, and open source materials can save them money!

98

Students benefit from open textbooks by providing the most up-to-date info. Just remember to balance that with context and collaboration.

99

Students benefit by paying lower costs for open textbooks and have opportunity to learn in a customized environment.

100

With open textbooks, students can choose their preferred format at the best price. More content at lower cost.

101

A printed textbook weights three pounds, but a world of knowledge via the Internet weighs nothing.

102

Students can receive email reminders with a link to the chapter they're supposed to read, which helps keep them on track for the course.

103

Open textbooks enhance faculty's ability to provide access to more original content in ways that promotes a student's interactive learning.

104

Accessibility to learning can be redefined by providing content in ways that support strengths such as a visual or auditory learning style.

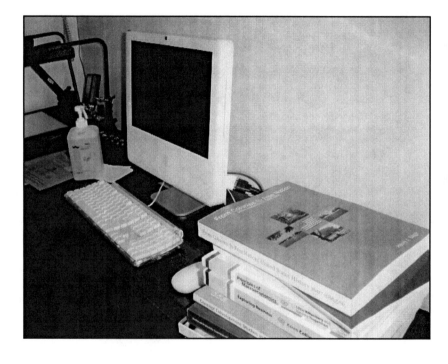

Section VII

Where Are We Headed?

The road ahead is full of promises and potholes. The goal has to be achieving success that is impactful and measureable on each target audience.

105

Good news! There is free access to many of Shakespeare's works! If only I'd had this in college, I could've saved so much money! :->

106

Open textbooks can fundamentally transform and unlock education by actively engaging all of us in the creation of our own learning content.

107

There is a growing trend towards building a world-class catalog of free and open college level textbooks.

108

Open access textbooks are another step in the direction of more collaborative, less hierarchical learning.

109

We could share our instructional digital resources—including courses, textbooks, and library resources—and use others' digital materials.

110

Publicly funded digital content =
openly licensed and freely available
content to those that paid for it.

111

We are headed towards educational
affordability and openness, where
quality content can be created, rated,
shared, and adapted by all.

112

There is a great future for open education resources. We need to embrace the concept that education is a fundamental right for all of us.

113

The future is not really free books, but we will have more nominally priced textbooks and many eBooks priced around $10 each.

114

With the rising costs of textbooks, many of which are over $100, students can no longer afford to buy them. We need an alternative.

115

This is our future—an increasingly open educational environment where content and resources are open freely for adoption and customization.

116

The future is about the open collaboration of both students and instructors to create reusable adopted open textbook content and resources.

117

We have a moral obligation to keep education accessible.

118

Hopefully, we are moving away from restrictive material, towards open, collaborative, constant exchange.

119

Share to learn ... learn to share.

120

General education will be free to all.

121

We need to be green when it comes to textbooks. Open textbooks promote sustainability and help to save the planet—one textbook at a time!

122

The impact of open textbook use is enhancing faculty's ability to support interactive learning processes. This is the future.

123

The increase in open textbook adoption is redefining the importance of faculty collaboration in streamlining learning content integration.

124

The growing trend and support for open textbooks has led to faculty taking on a more active advocacy role, which is a win-win for everyone.

125

There are a growing number of accessibility options, like Bookshare, with an online accessible library for people with print disabilities.

126

To grow the open textbook movement, we need to simplify the process of finding and adopting high-quality textbooks.

127

Thought leaders in open textbooks will lead the way in bringing high-quality content, advocacy training, and a community of shared experts.

128

Open textbook adoption will require a partnership between authors and publishers who can demonstrate marketing and distribution expertise.

129

Transforming teaching and learning using open textbooks is critical in this digital era if we are to have a competitive U.S. workforce.

130

Fair use only applies to U.S. copyrights; as open textbooks expand globally, we need to address all countries' copyright laws.

131

We need to offer students flexibility and affordability in their education options. Open textbooks need to be a part of the equation.

132

Availability of peer-reviewed open textbooks enables faculty to find high-quality content to include in their interactive learning process.

133

We need to address an increasing demand for open textbooks that provides flexibility and customization options for the right price.

134

To succeed with open textbooks, we need a sustainable model that supports an engaged and invested faculty- and student-user community.

135

The future can be defined by how successful we are with the implementation and increased access of open resources for students.

136

Injured veterans can access emerging virtual worlds that will support their learning disabilities, both physical and cognitive.

137

As technology evolves and grows so do the options for open textbooks.

138

Building on the dream that technology will evolve and change our vision of education is our hope for the future.

139

Converging high-quality educational content with emerging technology has made our future a brighter one.

140

The digital age is redefining how we learn, get information, and collaborate, engaging students in multiple ways. It is our future.

About the Author

Sharyn Fitzpatrick has over 25 years experience in sales and marketing including executive positions with The Learning Company, Knight-Ridder and Sum-Total Systems as well as principal of Marcom Gurus, a high-tech agency she founded in 2000, Her love for education has continued with her taking a leadership role on the College Open Textbooks marketing team.

Other Books in the THINKaha Series

The THINKaha book series is for thinking adults who lack the time or desire to read long books, but want to improve themselves with knowledge of the most up-to-date subjects. THINKaha is a leader in timely, cutting-edge books and mobile applications from relevant experts that provide valuable information in a fun, Twitter-brief format for a fast-paced world.

They are available online at http://thinkaha.com or at other online and physical bookstores.

1. *#BOOK TITLE tweet Book01*: 140 Bite-Sized Ideas for Compelling Article, Book, and Event Titles by Roger C. Parker

2. *#DEATHtweet Book01*: A Well Lived Life through 140 Perspectives on Death and its Teachings by Timothy Tosta

3. *#DIVERSITYtweet Book01*: Embracing the Growing Diversity in Our World by Deepika Bajaj

4. *#DREAMtweet Book01*: Inspirational Nuggets of Wisdom from a Rock and Roll Guru to Help You Live Your Dreams by Joe Heuer

5. *#ENTRYLEVELtweet Book01*: Taking Your Career from Classroom to Cubicle by Heather R. Huhman

6. *#JOBSEARCHtweet Book01*: 140 Job Search Nuggets for Managing Your Career and Landing Your Dream Job by Barbara Safani

7. *#LEADERSHIPtweet Book01*: 140 Bite-Sized Ideas to Help You Become the Leader You Were Born to Be by Kevin Eikenberry

8. *#MILLENNIALtweet Book01*: 140 Bite-sized Ideas for Managing the Millennials by Alexandra Levit

9. *#MOJOtweet*: 140 Bite-Sized Ideas on How to Get and Keep Your Mojo by Marshall Goldsmith

10. *#PARTNER tweet Book01*: 140 Bite-Sized Ideas for Succeeding in Your Partnerships by Chaitra Vedullapalli

#OPEN TEXTBOOK **tweet**

Breinigsville, PA USA
11 October 2010
247028BV00006B/1/P